HEREDITY:
ON!

REBECCA HIRSH

Rourke
Educational Media

rourkeeducationalmedia.com

Teaching Focus:

Have students locate the ending punctuation for sentences in the book. Count how many times a period, question mark, or exclamation point is used. Which one is used the most? What is the purpose for each ending punctuation mark? Practice reading these sentences with appropriate expression.

Before Reading:

Building Academic Vocabulary and Background Knowledge

Before reading a book, it is important to set the stage for your child or student by using pre-reading strategies. This will help them develop their vocabulary, increase their reading comprehension, and make connections across the curriculum.

1. Look at the cover of the book. What will this book be about?
2. What do you already know about the topic?
3. Let's study the Table of Contents. What will you learn about in the book's chapters?
4. What would you like to learn about this topic? Do you think you might learn about it from this book? Why or why not?
5. Use a reading journal to write about your knowledge of this topic. Record what you already know about the topic and what you hope to learn about the topic.
6. Read the book.
7. In your reading journal, record what you learned about the topic and your response to the book.
8. After reading the book complete the activities below.

Content Area Vocabulary

Read the list. What do these words mean?

combinations
environment
experiments
medieval
microscope
particle
pollen
resemble
surroundings
trait

After Reading:

Comprehension and Extension Activity

After reading the book, work on the following questions with your child or students to check their level of reading comprehension and content mastery.

1. What are some traits that polar bears inherit from their parents? (Summarize)
2. How does thick fur and large paws help a polar bear survive in its environment? (Infer)
3. In what ways are animals like their parents? How are they different? (Asking Questions)
4. What are some traits that you share with people in your family? What ways do you look different? (Text to Self Connection)
5. Why did Gregor Mendel reject the idea that traits from parents blended in their offspring? (Asking Questions)

Extension Activity

Trace your hand on a piece of construction paper. Cut out the hand. On each finger, write one trait that you have inherited. You can choose traits like eye color, hair color, curly or straight hair, dimples, freckles, and whether you can roll your tongue into a tube. You can make a hand for each person in your family. Draw a trunk on a large piece of paper or poster board. Glue or tape the hands above the trunk to form a tree.

Table of Contents

What Is Heredity?

Two polar bear cubs wrestle in the snow. Their mother watches. The cubs and their mother all look like each other. They all have thick, light-colored fur, four legs, and four big paws.

Offspring, or children, **resemble** others of their kind. We call this heredity. You can see heredity at work all around you. Puppies look like dogs, kittens look like cats, and human children look like grown-ups.

Unique You

You can see heredity at work in yourself. Eye color, hair color, freckles, dimples, and long eyelashes are all traits that were passed on to you from your parents.

Elephants Can't Have Mice

Heredity means that all animals give birth to their own kind. Bears have cubs, pigs have piglets, and people have baby humans. No elephant has ever given birth to baby mice!

Plants follow the rules of heredity too. Each plant makes more of its own kind. Oak trees make acorns, which grow into new oak trees. Bean plants make bean seeds, which grow into new bean plants.

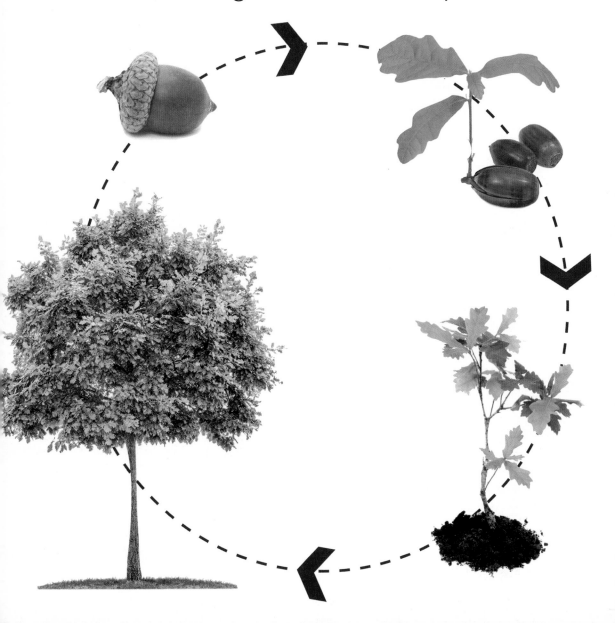

All living things inherit traits from their parents. A kitten inherits a long tail and pointy ears. A baby giraffe inherits patterned fur and a long neck. Oak trees inherit the shape of their leaves.

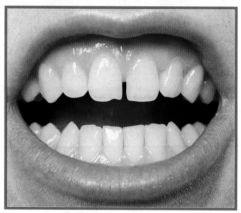

Inherited Traits

- Widow's peak
- Crooked little finger
- Tongue rolling
- Earlobe hangs free
- Front teeth have definite gap
- Second toe is longer than big toe

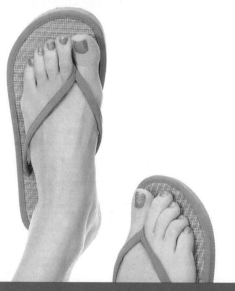

Inherited traits can help a living thing survive in its **environment**. Polar bears live in a frozen world of snow and ice. White fur helps them blend in with their **surroundings**. Large paws help them walk on the snow and ice.

So Long, Winter!
Many animals inherit behaviors called instincts. Some birds, like geese, have the instinct to fly south when winter is coming.

Some traits are shaped by the environment. An Arctic fox has white fur in winter to blend in with the snow and ice. During the summer, the fox's fur turns darker to blend in with the colors of fall and spring.

Each living thing is slightly different from others of its kind. Just as no two people look alike, every plant and animal is different. No two tigers have the same pattern of stripes. No two sunflower plants look exactly alike.

Look-Alikes

The only people that look alike are identical twins. Although they look identical, they are still unique because they are influenced by their experiences and their environments.

Even living things within a family are unique. Puppies in a litter look different, even though they have the same parents. One puppy may have sharper teeth and bigger ears than its brothers and sisters. One may be playful while another is shy.

Frogs from Slime

In **medieval** times, heredity was a mystery. People mistakenly believed that nonliving things could turn into animals. They thought frogs came from slime and flies came from rotten meat.

Life Cycle of a Fly

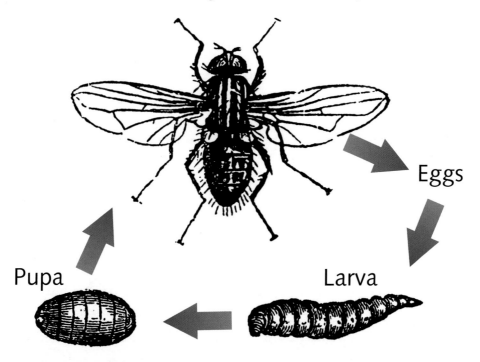

Eggs

Larva

Pupa

A Recipe for Mice

Medieval people thought that if you wrapped cheese and bread in rags and left it in a corner, you could make mice. What was really happening? Mice did appear in the rags, but it was because they had come to snack on the cheese!

Over time, people came to understand heredity better. Farmers learned they could cross, or mate, two kinds of sheep and create new sheep with thicker fur.

But the rules of heredity remained a mystery. People thought that traits blended like paints. Black paint mixed with white paint makes gray paint. People thought that a black cat father and a white cat mother would have gray kittens.

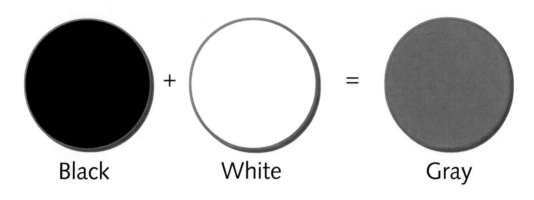

Black   +   White   =   Gray

But not all living things look like a blend of their parents. Sometimes, a black cat and a white cat would have white kittens. How could this happen? No one knew. No one had solved the mystery.

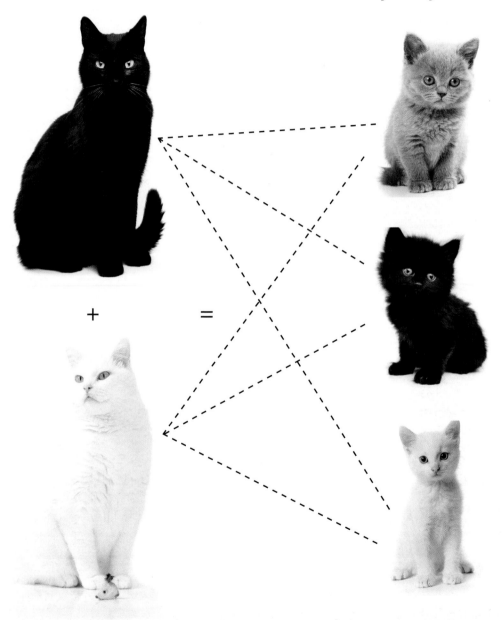

+ =

The Monk in the Garden

Gregor Mendel, a monk in Austria, wanted to understand heredity. He grew different kinds of pea plants in his garden. Some plants were tall and some were short. Some made white flowers and some made purple flowers. What would happen if he crossed, or mated, different pea plants?

Gregor crossed tall plants with short plants. He took **pollen** from the male part of a tall pea plant flower. He moved the pollen to the female part of a flower on a short pea plant. When he grew the baby plants, all of them were tall. None were short. The short **trait** had disappeared.

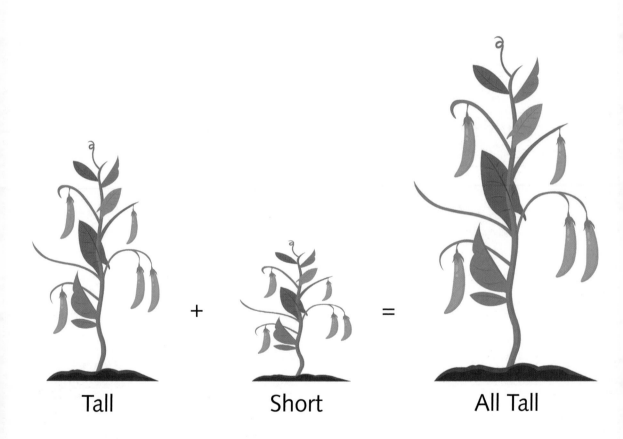

Tall   +   Short   =   All Tall

Then Gregor crossed the baby pea plants with each other, and grew more plants. Most of the new plants were tall, but one out of every four plants was short. The short trait had come back!

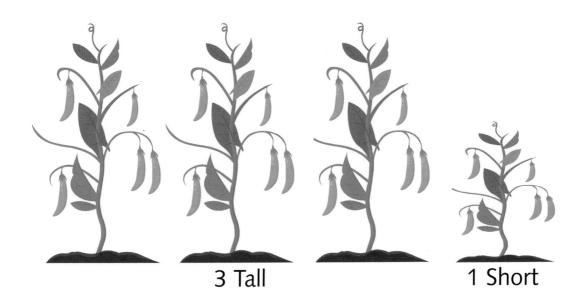

3 Tall   1 Short

Gregor the Scientist

As a monk, Gregor studied at the University of Vienna with some of the world's best scientists. His careful **experiments** required him to use a lot of math.

Gregor saw the same thing with other traits. He crossed pea plants that made purple flowers and pea plants that made white flowers. The result was all purple flowers. But if he crossed the new purple flowers to each other, about a fourth of the new plants made white flowers. The white trait had returned.

Mendel's Peas

Mendel studied seven different traits in pea plants:
- Pea shape (round or wrinkled)
- Pea color (green or yellow)
- Pod shape (constricted or inflated)
- Pod color (green or yellow)
- Flower color (purple or white)
- Plant size (tall or dwarf)
- Position of flowers (middle or end of stem)

He saw the same pattern of inheritance in all seven traits.

Gregor realized the traits weren't blending. Instead, each trait was passed on whole, like a **particle**. The tall parent passed on a particle for tallness. The short parent passed on a particle for shortness.

Pea Plant Characteristics

Trait	Dominant	Recessive
Stem Length	Tall	Short
Pod Shape	Inflated	Constricted
Seed Shape	Round	Wrinkled
Seed Color	Yellow	Green
Flower Position	Middle of Stem	End of Stem
Flower Color	Purple	White
Pod Color	Green	Yellow

These particles are called genes. A baby pea plant inherits one gene from each parent. Every gene comes in different forms, the way crayons come in different colors. The gene for height comes in two forms, a tall form and a short form.

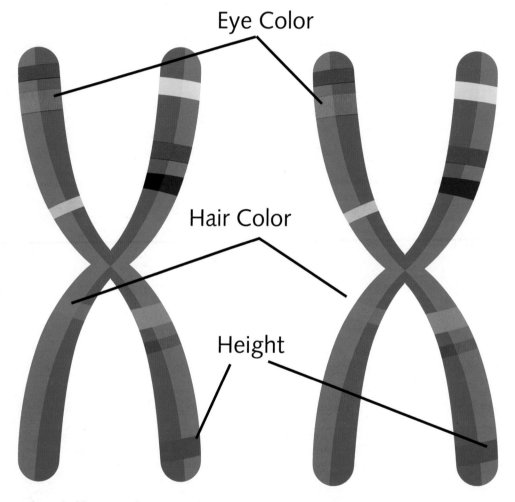

Eye Color

Hair Color

Height

The different forms of a gene are called alleles. Individual alleles control the inheritance of traits. Some alleles are dominant while other alleles are recessive.

Some traits are dominant, meaning strong. Other traits are recessive, or weak. The dominant trait covers up the recessive one. When a baby pea plant inherits one gene for tallness and one for shortness, all the baby plants are tall. Tallness is dominant.

Human Genes

Dominant:	Recessive:
Dark Hair	Light Hair
Curly Hair	Straight Hair
Brown Eyes	Light Color Eyes
Widow's Peak	Straight Hairline
Dimples	No Dimples
Unattached Ears	Attached Ears
Freckles	No Freckles
Broad Lips	Thin Lips

1822–1884

The Father of Heredity
Gregor Mendel published his ideas in 1866, but people did not notice. His ideas were rediscovered in 1900, long after his death. Now he is considered the "father of heredity."

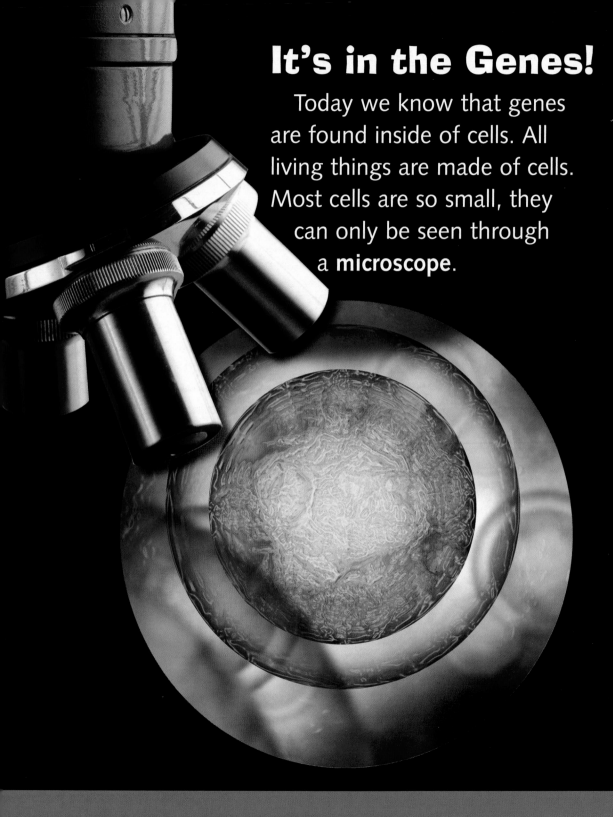

It's in the Genes!

Today we know that genes are found inside of cells. All living things are made of cells. Most cells are so small, they can only be seen through a **microscope**.

Inside every cell is a nucleus, or command center. Inside the nucleus are stringy objects called chromosomes. Chromosomes carry genes. The genes are lined up along the chromosomes, like beads on a string.

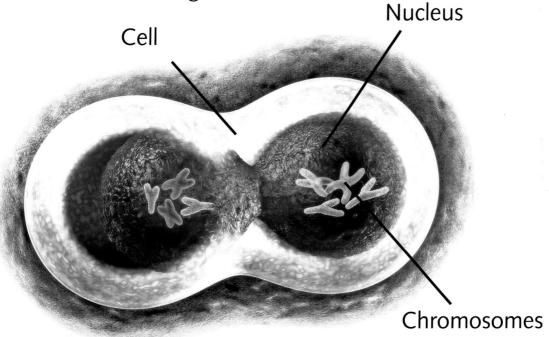

Cell

Nucleus

Chromosomes

1866–1945

Born in Bottles
Thomas Hunt Morgan showed that genes are on chromosomes through experiments with fruit flies raised in bottles. Fruit flies have giant chromosomes that can easily be seen with a microscope.

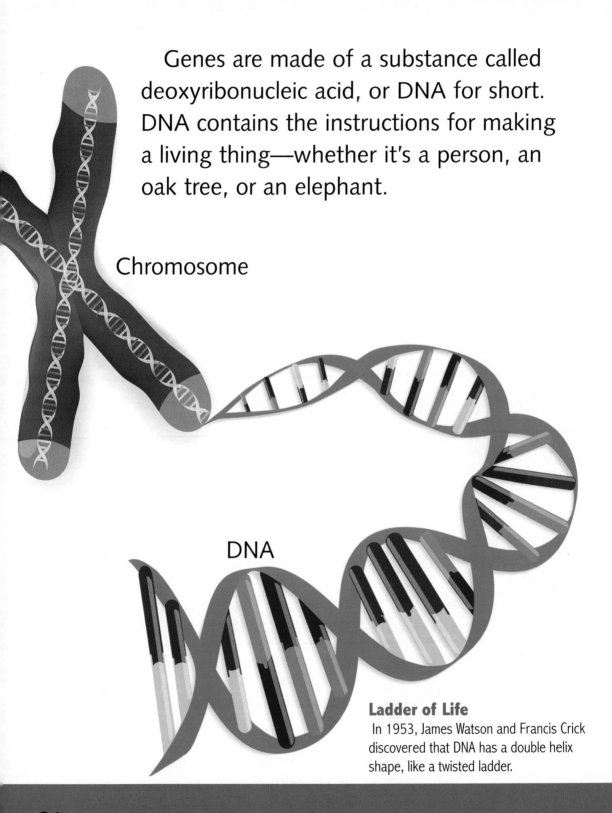

Genes are made of a substance called deoxyribonucleic acid, or DNA for short. DNA contains the instructions for making a living thing—whether it's a person, an oak tree, or an elephant.

Chromosome

DNA

Ladder of Life
In 1953, James Watson and Francis Crick discovered that DNA has a double helix shape, like a twisted ladder.

Slight changes in DNA result in different traits. These changes cause pea plants to grow tall or short. They cause dogs to have pointed ears or droopy ears. They cause people to have brown eyes or blue eyes.

Parents	Odds: Eye Color of the Baby		
● + ● =	● 75%	● 18.75%	● 6.25%
● + ● =	● 50%	● 37.5%	● 12.5%
● + ● =	● 50%	● 0%	● 50%
● + ● =	● <1%	● 75%	● 25%
● + ● =	● 0%	● 50%	● 50%
● + ● =	● 0%	● 1%	● 99%

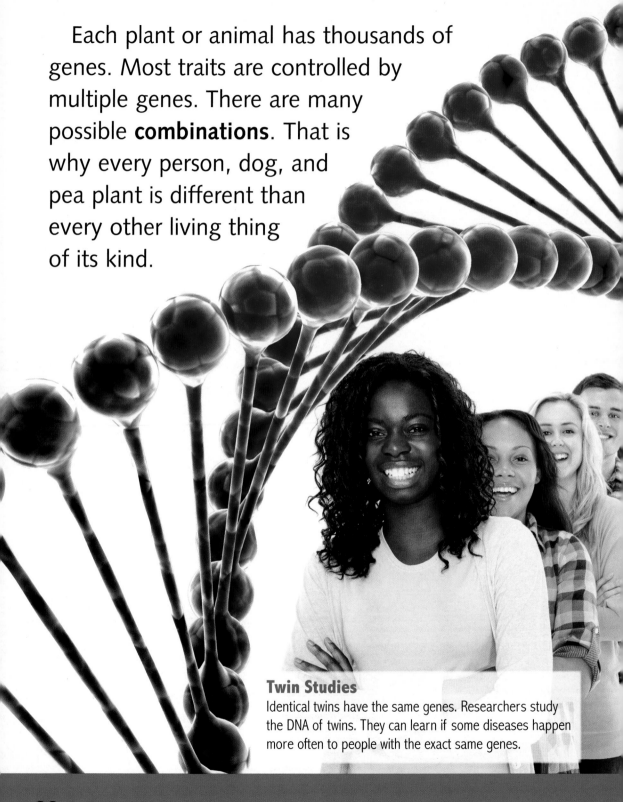

Each plant or animal has thousands of genes. Most traits are controlled by multiple genes. There are many possible **combinations**. That is why every person, dog, and pea plant is different than every other living thing of its kind.

Twin Studies

Identical twins have the same genes. Researchers study the DNA of twins. They can learn if some diseases happen more often to people with the exact same genes.

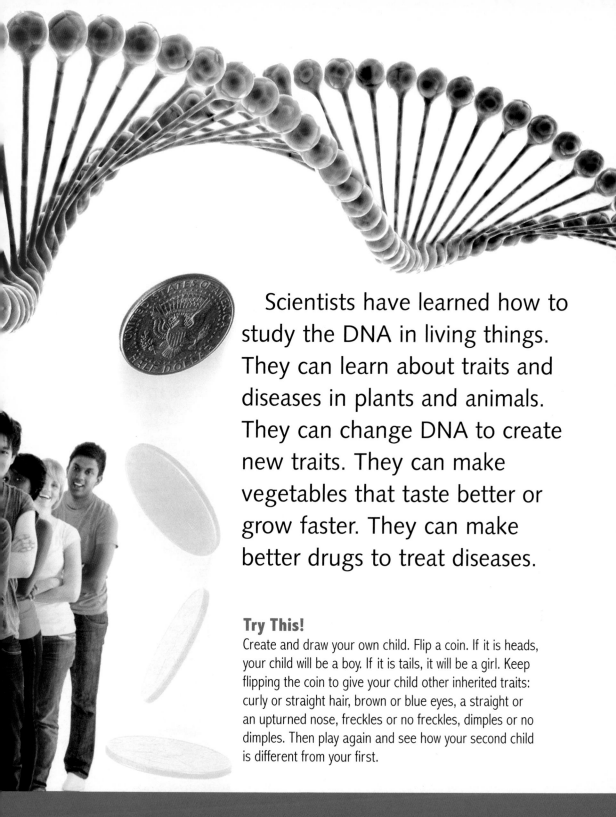

Scientists have learned how to study the DNA in living things. They can learn about traits and diseases in plants and animals. They can change DNA to create new traits. They can make vegetables that taste better or grow faster. They can make better drugs to treat diseases.

Try This!

Create and draw your own child. Flip a coin. If it is heads, your child will be a boy. If it is tails, it will be a girl. Keep flipping the coin to give your child other inherited traits: curly or straight hair, brown or blue eyes, a straight or an upturned nose, freckles or no freckles, dimples or no dimples. Then play again and see how your second child is different from your first.

Glossary

combinations (kahm-buh-NAY-shuhns): the results of mixing together a large number of parts

environment (in-VEYE-ruhn-muhnt): the conditions that surround and influence the form of a plant or animal and its ability to survive

experiments (ik-SPEER-uh-muhnts): a series of careful steps carried out to discover something

medieval (mee-DEE-vuhl): relating to the Middle Ages, from the fifth to the fifteenth century

microscope (MEYE-kruh-skohp): an instrument that uses a lens or lenses to make enlarged images of very small objects

particle (PAHRT-i-kuhl): a very small piece of matter

pollen (PAWL-uhn): tiny, dust-like particles from a flower that fertilize the seeds

resemble (ri-ZEM-buhl): to be like or similar to

surroundings (suh-ROUN-dingz): the conditions and objects that surround a living thing

trait (trayt): a feature that is inherited

Index

Show What You Know

1. How do the traits of a polar bear help it survive in its surroundings?

2. What mistaken belief did people in medieval times hold about heredity?

3. What living thing did Gregor Mendel use for his heredity experiments?

4. What did Gregor Mendel discover about dominant and recessive genes?

5. Where in the cell are genes and chromosomes located?

Websites to Visit

www.amnh.org/explore/ology/genetics

http://learn.genetics.utah.edu/content/basics

https://unlockinglifescode.org/timeline?tid=4

About the Author

Rebecca Hirsch grew up climbing trees and splashing in streams in her home state of Pennsylvania. She holds a Ph.D. in biology, and her writing draws on her love of the natural world and her background as a working scientist. Her books have been chosen as Junior Library Guild Selections and been named to "best of" reading lists. Rebecca lives with her husband and three children in the mountains of central Pennsylvania, where she still loves to climb trees and splash in streams. Visit her online at rebeccahirsch.com.

Meet The Author!
www.meetREMauthors.com

www.rourkeeducationalmedia.com

PHOTO CREDITS: Cover and title page: ©Rawpixerl Ltd; table of contents: ©kristen sekulic; p.4: ©Paulina Lenting-Smulders; p.5: ©Zagorodnaya, ©Art Marie; p.6: ©Anthony Gaudio, ©monkeybusinessimages, ©LuCaAr; p.7: ©subjug, ©AndriiM, ©redmal, ©Zerbor; p.8: ©Ozgur Coskun, ©Ocskay Bence, ©Nobilior; p.9: ©Justinreznick, ©CreativeNature_nl; p.10: ©Dmitry Deshevykh, ©zanskar; p.11: ©Richard Upshur; p.12: ©Liliya Kulianionak; p.12: ©oilbusca, ©Sebastian Duda; p.14: ©vicuschka; p.15, 16: ©Antagain, ©JLVarga, ©Dixi_; p.16: ©Bart_Kowski, ©Frans Rombout; p.17: ©Alter_photo, ©Milenakatzer; p.19: ©meshaphoto; p.20: ©chengyuzheng; p.21: ©olgaserova; p.24: ©SERDAR YAGCI, ©ClaudioVentrella; p.25: ©man_at_mouse, ©rob_lan; p.26: ©ttsz; p.28-29: ©Jezperklauzen, ©Dean Mitchell; p.29: ©jgroup

Edited by: Keli Sipperley
Cover design by: Rhea Magaro-Wallace
Interior design by: Kathy Walsh

Library of Congress PCN Data

Heredity: Pass It On! / Rebecca Hirsh
(Science Alliance)
ISBN 978-1-68342-348-5 (hard cover)
ISBN 978-1-68342-444-4 (soft cover)
ISBN 978-1-68342-514-4 (e-Book)
Library of Congress Control Number: 2017931192

Rourke Educational Media
Printed in the United States of America,
North Mankato, Minnesota